-NO-
WORRIES

NO WORRIES

HOW TO CALM AN
ANXIOUS MIND

DR ASHLEY CONWAY

First published in ebook in 2015 as
*Therapy Toolkit: A Short Book on Anxiety
and Panic Attacks (and how to beat them)*
by Short Books
an imprint of Octopus Publishing Group Ltd
Carmelite House, 50 Victoria Embankment
London, EC4Y 0DZ

www.octopusbooks.co.uk
www.shortbooks.co.uk

An Hachette UK Company
www.hachette.co.uk

This updated print edition published in 2017
by Short Books

10 9 8 7 6 5 4 3 2

A CIP catalogue record for this book
is available from the British Library.

ISBN 978-1-78072-341-9

Cover design by Paul Bougourd

Printed and bound in Great Britain by Clays Ltd, Elcograf S.p.A.

This FSC® label means that materials used for the
product have been responsibly sourced

MIX
Paper from
responsible sources
FSC® C104740

In this short book, I am writing to provide information, illustration and hopefully some help. It does not constitute specific advice. If you are concerned about physical or psychological symptoms, please contact your medical practitioner or a qualified mental health advisor.

Contents

INTRODUCTION

IN THE 25 YEARS I have worked as a psychologist, I've seen huge developments in the ways my profession has helped people cope with the problems they face. Interestingly, though, it's not just the psychologists' models that have changed, but also the kinds of problems that our clients present with and the number of people seeking assistance.

Of course, when looking at such trends, it's not always easy to tell whether the incidence of a problem is increasing in real terms, or whether it simply appears that way because nowadays people are more likely to discuss it, and to seek support for it, than they used to be. My belief, however, is that when it comes to anxiety, the problem is genuinely on the increase, in terms of incidence and severity.

But why is this? There are probably numerous causes, but I believe that two particularly significant factors are (i) the way that we communicate now, and (ii) something that psychologists refer to as "conditionality".

In terms of communication, it seems to me that the more technology we use to keep in touch with the world, the less time we have available to actually talk to each other. Added to this, the more we are being sold a fantasy in our online lives, the less we are engaged in what is real. What's more, the quality of our communication is being reduced by the use of short bursts of words and abbreviations. After all, we now even have heads of state using less than 280 characters as a primary form of communication with the world. Is this a good way to deepen relationships? And does it improve our ability to understand what is going on in the world around us?

Human beings are social animals, yet we seem to be losing our way of making real contact with others. We have to be cool teenagers, great parents, have successful jobs and keep our children constantly occupied and entertained with activities that we think will improve their chances. The competition is fierce. Daily life has become threatening. We continually feel forced to ask ourselves, "Am I good enough?"

And this leads to the second point I mentioned: *conditionality*. If we are held in high regard and liked or loved by our friends and family for who we are, we experience the benefit of what is known as *unconditional* regard, being liked or loved *unconditionally* – which will generally enhance a feeling of wellbeing.

But if we can only feel OK about ourselves if we own the latest phone, wear the right labels and have a perfect body, our feeling of security is *conditional*. Consequently, if we can't have these things, or we lose them, we are likely to feel less secure and more anxious. To compound these issues, we live in a time that is pro-positivity – for some reason we are not allowed to express feelings of sadness, doubt or fear. Employers and friends seem to want us to be happy all the time.

It's this constant self-doubt, I think, that has

become much worse over the last two decades, and as a result the invisible scourge of insecurity and anxiety has increased in people of all ages and cultures. Anxiety may not be as easily observable as a limp, or an arm in a sling, but it is highly pervasive and can be severely disruptive to the people living with it.

But – and finally we get to the good part – there is a solution. Anxiety can be overcome. We can apply a whole range of strategies to reduce and even eliminate anxiety, and live happy, confident, healthy lives.

What is anxiety?

Anxiety is often thought to have the same emotional basis as fear, but there are key differences in these two states of being. Fear is the emotional response to a real or perceived imminent threat. Anxiety is the anticipation of some negative future event (which may or may not be specific). It is worrying even when there is nothing objectively wrong, or to a level that is disproportionate to the actual risk. It may involve spending a lot of waking hours dwelling upon something, and seeking frequent reassurance from others. The focus of the worry may shift from one thing to another – for example from one's own health or wellbeing to the health of loved ones, or to work or finances.

Anxiety functions in a loop between the mind and the body. Negative thoughts can trigger adverse physical reactions, and those reactions can trigger worrying thoughts (*Have I got something wrong with me? Am I ill? Losing the plot?*). These thoughts can, in turn, trigger further physical reactions, and so the vicious cycle progresses.

What psychologists call an anxiety disorder involves excessive anxiety and worry, apprehensive expectation and a tendency to catastrophise about a variety of events or activities. People talk about a feeling of dread or impending doom and experience a range of physical symptoms – feeling restless, on edge or irritable, getting easily tired, having difficulty concentrating or finding their minds going blank, depersonalisation (feeling detached from themselves, almost as if they were observing a movie of their actions), derealisation (feeling detached from the world, experiencing others and their environment as if it were unreal) and the desire to escape from the place or situation that they find themselves in. It sounds almost unbelievable that our minds can do this to us, but as I will outline in this book, this response is the consequence of a mechanism developed through evolution that can become maladaptive in our modern world. The individual finds it difficult to control the worry symptoms, which may be accompanied by physical sensations, including increased sweating, feeling fidgety or hot, sleep disturbances, muscle tension, faster breathing, trembling, a feeling of the heart pounding hard or quickly, dizziness or lightheadedness, and digestive tract irregularities. No wonder, then, that anxiety can cause such distress, and interferes to such a degree in people's social and work lives.

What are the causes?

I believe that two major factors increase the likelihood of anxiety: a feeling of helplessness (i.e. of not being in control) and a lack of predictability. We can't help but notice that, on a macro level, the world is going through rapid change in unprecedented ways. Some of the factors that, in the past, would have helped maintain a sense of stability and constancy – the extended family, religion, faith in our political systems, a sense of safety in the order of the world – are often no longer there. Now, increasing urbanisation leads to overcrowding, which may in itself raise our stress levels, and although we may have millions of people around us, we seem to have lost a sense of community and feel more alone and isolated. Jobs feel less secure, and while a generation ago they began and ended in the workplace, now, with 24-hour access to communication and global working patterns, the boundaries between what is work time and what is downtime are increasingly blurred. Perceived wealth gaps (whether real or not) create further tensions in our society. On top of all of this, people's attempts to cope with a demanding world by using recreational drugs and alcohol only make matters worse, and taking stimulants, such as caffeine or "energy" drinks, to overcome the after-effects of such substance use can then further escalate the problem.

Modern technology may have improved our lives in many ways, yet I can't help but feel that it has also created just as many problems – social media, for instance, connects us with friends and family like never before, right across the globe, but it brings with it new kinds of pressures that we are not used to. An obvious example is the harm inflicted by online bullying and stalking, abuse generated and recycled, scams and threats and deceptions. Perhaps less obvious is the stress caused by being bombarded with images of what our bodies *should* look like, what labels we *should* be wearing, what food we *should* be eating and how successful we *should* be. The medium is widely used by people to promote narcissistic images of themselves as glamorous, successful and super-happy, scrubbing clean the other, supposedly less attractive aspects of their lives. This creates an environment in which some people feel inadequate and even more isolated, as if, in some way, they are missing out.

All these changes and increasing demands upon our time and attention create the ideal conditions for an alarm response in the mind and the body. This so-called "fight or flight" response is a normal animal reaction to a perceived threat – but it is a behaviour left over from evolutionary adaptation. The conditions under which this response is appropriate are: when the threat is literal (i.e. a physical threat to our life or personal safety); when the necessary response is physical (i.e. fighting or running away); and when the timing is immediate (i.e. the response is required now, and there is an endpoint at which the danger will be over).

It is rare that a threat in the modern world will follow this blueprint. These days, most perceived threats that we face are not usually a threat to our lives, but possibly to our sense of wellbeing – a threat of losing our job, concern over whether our children are happy, what will happen to us in old age and so on. The appropriate response is not physical, the threat is often not immediate (concerning, as it does, what might happen in the future) and there is often no clear endpoint to the worry. So we are left with an evolutionary response to a threat that is no longer appropriate to the world in which we live. This continuous state of inappropriate alarm can often lead to persistent feelings of anxiety.

How can we heal?

The good news is the situation is not hopeless! In this book we'll look at strategies for dealing with anxiety and panic attacks, covering the four main categories that I address whenever somebody comes to see me with such concerns. These are:

1) Physiological
   The mind and the body are inextricably linked, and physiological changes go a long way to benefiting the mind. Exercise is good for reducing anxiety, but then there must also be a balance, with time for relaxation and quality sleep.

   Eating regularly and sensibly, avoiding stimulants like caffeine and not overdoing alcohol all help. Breathing techniques – which will be covered in this book – can be invaluable in helping quieten the body and mind.

2) Cognitive
   We must challenge negative thinking patterns. Recognising which issues in your

life you can do something about will help you focus on the productive action you can take and help you let go of the counter-productive worries about things over which you have no control. Reminding yourself that most of the things that cause you stress are irritations rather than catastrophes is a simple but effective skill.

Mindfulness techniques, so popular these days, can really help quieten the mind.

3) <u>Behavioural</u>
Don't do avoidance. Do not withdraw from the world. Go out and engage with people. You will find approaches to this strategy in the "healing" sections of this book.

4) <u>Emotional</u>
These days, more than ever, it is important that we prioritise time with loved ones and friends. Research shows that talking about our true feelings to an empathic listener is good for us. Be real. Be yourself. Do not live your life according to the measures of others. Pay attention to what truly satisfies

your heart. In this way, you will like who you are – and as a result be less likely to feel anxious.

Using this book

In this book two stories are told: of Michelle, who suffered from an anxiety disorder, and of Peter, who struggled with panic attacks and agoraphobia. Neither story is about an actual person; both are works of fiction. But both are accurate portrayals of the kind of thing that does happen to real people, and are based on my years of experience in dealing with individuals who have worked through their problems and recovered from periods in their lives when they have suffered from anxiety and panic attacks. I hope their stories serve as guidance and inspiration in times of difficulty, and reassure you that there is always a way through to a more peaceful life.

In this book I will take a closer look at what anxiety is, offer tips and ideas for healing, and provide a summary of each section to highlight the key issues.

If you are reading this because you are

suffering from anxiety or panic, or to help a loved one, I wish you well. The path is not always easy, but recovery is achievable. It helps to be understanding and have patience, with both yourself and others.

I hope that this book helps you along your journey.

PART ONE

CHAPTER 1

WHAT IS AN ANXIETY DISORDER?

MICHELLE'S STORY

MICHELLE WAS A WORRIER. SOMETIMES it felt to her that she had spent her whole life worrying. She remembered as a child she would worry that something bad would happen to her mother – that she would get ill and die, or else have an accident when Michelle was at school. Her mother never did have any serious illnesses or accidents, but the evidence did not seem to make any difference to the young Michelle – she just worried. She was a bright girl, but would always be anxious approaching any kind of assessment. She would work hard revising and often not sleep well the night before an exam. When she came out she would think of all of the things that she should have written, and how she had let herself down. But she always did well. Again, the evidence did not seem to make a lot of difference to her expectations. Even as she got older she would always underestimate her performance in assessments and be concerned that she had done badly. At school, although not one of the most popular children, she acquired a small group of close friends – friendships that would remain into her adulthood. Her sensitivity, which was often the source of her angst, was also a gift in her friendships. She would often accurately perceive what her friend was feeling, and be thoughtful, caring and responsive.

As she grew up she realised that she did not like cocktail-party chatter. She was not comfortable with flitting from one conversation to another with different people, as some of her more confident friends seemed to do with ease. After social events Michelle would often go home and worry that she had said the wrong thing, or talked too much, or too little, or had offended someone in some way. She would pick over elements of the event in her mind and cringe inwardly at the thought of her own behaviour.

She was an attractive girl, but her lack of self-confidence often inhibited her relationships with boys. She could never quite understand why they might be interested in her. But when she was eighteen she met Patrick, an intelligent, quiet, sensitive boy of her own age, and they seemed just right for each other. Then she got a job as an office junior with a firm of accountants in Reading, and he went off to university in Bristol to study economics. They were only 80 miles apart, and they saw each other regularly – either he came back to see her at home or she travelled up to Bristol on a Friday night after work, returning late on Sunday. People thought that their relationship would not last through university, but Michelle and Patrick had no doubts – and last it did. It was not so much that Michelle dreamed of marrying Patrick, but simply that it seemed like the most obvious and natural course of events.

Patrick had not had a gap year between

school and university, so after graduating he decided that he wanted to go travelling before looking for a full-time job. He had a couple of friends from university who were interested in going with him, and he asked Michelle if she wanted to come too. She thought about it, and told him that it would be more sensible for her to carry on living with her parents, and to save some money while he was away. She shyly told him that she would like them to move into a flat together when he was back, and he said that he would love to, and kissed her. Looking back, she often wondered what it was that really made her say no to going. Was it what she'd said, or was it that she was anxious about all those aeroplane journeys, strange countries and scary places? She also wondered how much the course of her life would have changed if she'd have said yes to him, if she'd have gone on that trip. But maybe it would have ended in the same way whatever she'd done.

His trip took place at the beginning of the internet age, and this meant that they were able to stay in touch by e-mail, which was very new at the time. They also had occasional telephone conversations, when Michelle would hear about his adventures, and she would tell him about how her family was, and what was going on in Reading.

It was towards the end of his trip that she started to feel the anxiety growing. The calls seemed to be more spaced out in time. They seemed shorter. He sounded less excited to speak to her. There seemed to be reasons why he had to go. The e-mails seemed less affectionate. Something was wrong. She couldn't tell what – but something was wrong.

They had arranged for her to pick him up from Heathrow when he was due to arrive back home. She waited at the arrivals point and watched as more and more people from his flight wrapped themselves in the arms of loved ones. She waited and waited. Then she saw him. He looked stressed. "They've lost my bag," he said as he approached her.

"Oh, sorry to hear that. I'm sure it'll turn up," she replied and opened her arms to him. His hug did not feel right. Maybe it was tiredness. Maybe it was jetlag. Maybe it was something else. They walked to her car in silence punctuated by odd polite exchanges.

"So how was the flight?"

"Good, yeah, fine."

"And you're well?"

"Yeah, fine. You?"

Three or four junctions west of Heathrow, Michelle surprised Patrick by pulling off at an exit and parking in a side road (in fact she rather surprised herself with this action, which seemed to come from somewhere deep in her unconscious). Once she had put on the handbrake and switched off the engine, she knew what she had to ask. It was not courage that enabled her to do it, but a terrible, nagging, consuming anxiety that was unbearable. It gave her no choice.

"So what's going on?" she asked.

"What do you mean?"

"Something is going on. There's something wrong. Tell me what it is." Michelle's words sounded strong, but her voice was trembling.

He told her. He'd met someone six weeks before. In Machu Pichu. She was just sitting there on a rock smoking a joint and watching the sunset. He stared at her because she looked so laid back. She called him over and offered him a toke, and for the first time in his life he took one. It was amazing. She was called

Shanti, which means "the tranquil one" and she was very beautiful. They had been together every day since. He supposed that she was what some people would call a hippy, but she didn't like labels, and nor did he. He assured Michelle that Shanti was a really nice person, and that if she met her she would really like her; everybody did. She was Australian by birth, but she was an amazing mix of everything – her dad was a Hindu, and her mother was Danish, and that's probably where she gets her distinctive looks from. And she was on her way back to Australia, and she was going to set up an organic food café in Byron Bay. And she had asked him to come and be part of it. And he had said yes. "Sorry. I didn't want to tell you over the phone, and I wanted to be sure. But when I left her, and flying back, thinking about it, I just know it's the right thing. It's what I have to do. It's what I'm *meant* to do."

Michelle said very little, and made barely a sound as the tears rolled down her cheeks. She nodded, and switched the engine back on and drove back to Reading. She dropped Patrick off at his parents' house. He asked if he should give her a call the next day. She shook her head in silence, and when he leaned forward to give her a kiss goodbye, she turned her wet cheek to him while her arms dangled at her sides.

When she got home, her parents could see that she was distressed. When they asked her what was wrong she said simply, "Peter's going to Australia to live with a girl. She's called Shanti. It means 'the tranquil one'. She's very beautiful, and a really nice person. And she's very laid back, and everyone likes her." Then she went up to her room.

That night she tossed and turned, thoughts and questions whirring through her mind. Should she have gone on the trip? Why wasn't she laid back? Was she a boring person with a boring job? Living with boring parents, living in a boring town? She was sure she was not sexy or good-looking, so why would a man want to stay with her? She was desperately hurt and upset. But she didn't really blame Patrick. He could have a much more exciting life with someone else.

In the early hours she gave up trying to sleep, and got up. She went downstairs and put the kettle on. Her stomach was hurting. She went to the loo and had diarrhoea.

It was just the beginning. Over the next few months the gut problems became worse, and she found herself needing to go to the toilet five or six times a day. Eventually, after she had frightened herself by passing some blood, she went to the doctor. Her GP listened to her and examined her, and told her that she had Irritable Bowel Syndrome (IBS), and that the bleeding was caused by a haemorrhoid which was itself the result of strain and spasm in her colon. She was told that IBS was frequently associated with stress.

Michelle had a pretty healthy diet, but the consultant told her to eat more roughage and recommended plenty of wheat bran. Michelle did what she was told, but got more and more ill. After a number of months a friend suggested that she try leaving out wheat for a while. She did the experiment and it seemed to work. Somehow she turned this into a negative perception about herself. She was dumped by her boyfriend, then got IBS, then developed an allergy that she had never had before. How rubbish was she?

Michelle continued to work at the accountancy firm for the next decade, rising to the position of senior administration officer. She dated a few men, but the relationships did not progress. At work she rarely made mistakes, but worried about things that might be wrong. She worried that she might put something in the wrong file, or send an e-mail to the wrong person or get some information wrong for a client. She worried about the washing machine leaking and flooding the kitchen while she was at work, although nothing like this ever happened. She worried that something terrible would happen if she were late for an appointment, so she was rarely late – and, on the occasions when she was, nothing bad ever came of it. She worried about her parents being ill, despite the fact that they were both very healthy.

These concerns frequently caused her sleep to be disturbed. This meant that she was often tired, and felt that her concentration was not at its best. This made her fear that she would make a mistake, which in turn led to another disturbed night, thus maintaining a vicious circle.

She did not like to travel abroad. It was not simply a fear of flying, or more specifically a fear of crashing; it was all sorts of other anxieties: what if she were ill on the plane and needed to get off after it had taken off? What if she were ill while she was abroad? What if she had an accident? What if she lost her passport? Or her return ticket home? What if she were robbed and had no money? What if there were some rioting there? Or some terrorist attack? Or a flood? And on and on. What if? What if? What if? This meant that she did not go on holiday with her group of close friends when she was invited, and her little world shrunk even further. She was aware that her worry was excessive, but like a spider-phobe being told that spiders do not hurt you, this awareness made little difference to her. Unexpected noises would make her jump and wonder anxiously about their source. Once the anxious thoughts took hold they seemed to have a life of their own, and they would influence many of her major life decisions. She could not even imagine moving away from her parents or changing jobs – that would involve far too many uncertainties.

If she was questioned about something at work she could feel herself getting more and more tense, even if she knew the answer. When things got really bad her hands would shake. She was concerned about what people might think of her if they saw the trembling, and this just made her feel worse. Sometimes she would arrive home from work and feel her back, neck and shoulders locked up with tension. The IBS would wax and wane; sometimes she thought that she was free of it, and then, usually when she was really anxious, it would return to remind her what a tense person she was. She felt trapped in a continuous cycle, something from which she feared she would never be free.

Several factors led Michelle towards her anxiety disorder, from an existing tendency towards worry, to some specific triggers. She was a sensitive young woman, and she always seemed to have negative expectations about her actions. This affected her self-confidence and she often ended up feeling responsible for events that were not in her control, frequently blaming herself for anything that went wrong. As a result, she became increasingly fearful of doing anything. She was not receptive to evidence that challenged these negative beliefs about herself. She became more and more anxious, and developed physical symptoms of tension, such as irritable bowel syndrome. She reached a point where she would avoid going out into the world and she feared that she would never get better.

People with anxiety disorders may experience some or all of the same symptoms as Michelle, with a range of outside factors, such as personal history and life events, acting as triggers.

In the summary points we'll look at the symptoms of such a disorder, and later in the book we will see the methods Michelle used, under the guidance of a therapist, to become a much happier and more confident person.

Summary of Chapter 1
What is an anxiety disorder?

- The worries associated with an anxiety disorder can be difficult to control.

- Individuals with an anxiety disorder experience worry more severely and are more distressed by it than other people in similar circumstances, who might see their reaction as disproportionate to actual events.

- The worries are often about "what ifs?" i.e. things that have not actually happened.

- The anxiety may interfere with the work and/or personal life of the individual.

- The worries last longer and occur more frequently than they do for other people, and sometimes they may appear without any obvious trigger.

- Individuals with an anxiety disorder

frequently worry about things across a whole range of aspects of their lives.

- Physically, this kind of anxiety problem is often associated with tension, sometimes with shaking. Digestive tract problems (such as nausea and IBS) are quite common, and some individuals may experience increased sweating.

- Psychologically, this kind of anxiety is associated with poor sleep, tiredness and fatigue, feeling on edge, and experiencing difficulty concentrating. Some people find that the ongoing anxiety can make them irritable, and what psychologists call "an exaggerated startle response" (being jumpy) is common.

- Anxiety problems often get worse in times of stress.

- As we will see, there are methods for dealing with an anxiety disorder, and for managing instances of extreme worry.

CHAPTER 2

WHAT IS A PANIC ATTACK?

PETER'S STORY

PETER WAS NOT A NATURAL academic. At school he had a hard time achieving the necessary results at sixteen to enable him to carry on his education. At eighteen, soon after the death of his paternal grandmother, he left school with two low grades in his A-levels, having struggled with his exams.

It was a relief to be out of the education system, and he looked forward to getting into the world of work. He was an only child, and continued to live with his parents for the next few years. His father was a quiet, polite man, with no ambition, and his mother rather timid and afraid of the world, most comfortable staying at home with her little family, or perhaps inviting her sister and her family over for an occasional Sunday lunch. She always seemed to admire Peter's confidence: he went out with his friends and joined the local football club. He appeared to have such a busy social life, something she could not imagine for herself.

In fact, Peter had a natural talent with people. He was very sensitive, and always seemed to know in a moment what other people were feeling. He was not aware that this was unusual, or that he had any special talent; he assumed that everybody could do the same thing.

He got his first job working for one of the UK's largest double-glazing companies, in sales – the sharpest edge of the glass business, they always joked. As a trainee he received a tiny wage, and traipsed about with a variety of older salesmen to learn the ropes. But he learned much more than how to talk about windows

and doors and conservatories. He observed –
even though he was almost always unaware that
he was doing this. His friends, who thought
that they had more interesting jobs, would
tease him, but he made no secret of the fact
that he liked what he did, that it fascinated him.

He watched the salesmen at work. There
were a number of different types – those who
would bully and bludgeon until they got the
signature on the dotted line, and those who
would try to ingratiate themselves and charm
the customers. Others would mock the products of rival companies, and imply that the
customer would be foolish to go with anyone
else. And he watched the reaction of the
customers. Those that were timid and could be
bullied, those that were belligerent and closed
down, those that were pensive and wanted time
to think, and those that were impulsive and
would just blurt yes or no. He came to realise
that the outcome of this process was not usually
determined by price. It was about the quality of
the communication between the salesman and
the customer.

He learned quickly. The salesmen would
often resent having to take a trainee on their

trips, but Peter was liked universally. He was good company, and asked lots of questions. This made the salesmen feel knowledgeable and important. One of the observations that Peter made was regarding repeat business. He was interested in where a new contact came from. He noticed that the slower, more thoughtful salesmen tended to get more leads through referral from previous customers, whereas the bullying type might land a good one-off sale, possibly at an inflated price, but they rarely got repeat business.

After six months he was made a full-time salesman, his "trainee" title dropped. His salary was still very modest, but he was to be paid commission, which could give him a respectable income. He was set a target for his first year, which his boss told him was easily achievable in the patch of suburbia he would be covering.

He knew which type of salesman he wanted to be. He wanted repeat business. When he went out to see customers he would ask them questions, and listen to their answers. He always listened. Often he would leave the customer his card and say, "Have a think about it, and get back to me when you have made up your mind." The customers would often be surprised at the absence of a hard sell.

After six months, his boss called him in and cautioned him that his sales were not on target for the year. He had only achieved about 30 per cent of the year's goal in six months. That meant that he would have to make 70 per cent in the next six months. Peter was polite and acknowledged his boss's concerns, but said that he thought that he would be OK. There was something about his quiet confidence that softened his boss, who agreed to wait and see.

In fact, in his first year, Peter just made his target, and everybody seemed happy with that. His employers saw him as a bit of a slow starter, but now he seemed OK. At the end of the second year they realised that they had got it wrong. He was not just OK – he ended up achieving sales that were a little over *double* his target. It turned out he was something special. He had a gift. At only 21 he was already taking trainees out with him.

At 25 years old he was made a local manager, and three years after that he was promoted to regional manager. He loved the energy, the drive, the buzz he got from working with his sales teams. But there were two parts of his success that he did not much like. One was the increasing burden of paperwork that his promotions brought him. The second was giving presentations. As his career advanced, he became aware that he was comfortable with almost everybody, but when it came to giving formal presentations to the big bosses in their smart suits, he got nervous. Because of this discomfort he always prepared immensely well, made sure that he had all avenues covered, and that his talk would be interesting and stimulating to those present. Ironically, this diligence meant that he was considered a very good presenter by his company, and consequently was often the first choice for such tasks.

The company, meanwhile, had decided to keep up with the times and diversify, adding solar panels to their product list. It was a natural choice – the existing sales teams could be trained to promote these products when they were pitching for double-glazing, and the practicalities and logistics were very similar to what they were used to. Peter was excited about the idea too.

An important meeting was coming up, to be attended by the CEO and all the regional managers. Peter's boss called him into his office and asked him to make a presentation about a programme for training the existing salesmen in understanding the new product, and in how to sell it. It just so happened that, later that same day, Peter heard that his remaining grandmother, whose health had been in steady decline, had finally passed away. Although he had been very fond of her and was upset about her death, he pushed this feeling to the back of his mind to focus on the task at hand.

Now he had to force his attention onto the two things about his job that he did not like – he had to make a presentation to the directors, and to do that he would have to take some considerable time to plan it out on paper. He sat down at his keyboard, and began plodding through a strategy. He had to think about the desired endpoint, and then work backwards in terms of how to get there. Only then could he actually begin to plan his talk. To reach the endpoint he had to get a bunch of hard-nosed salesmen to take days out to attend training courses with one of the manufacturer's representatives. That meant they would be losing valuable commission-earning time. He would have to really sell it to them. That would probably be OK, he thought, because the carrot was the higher money-earning potential from being able to sell an additional product. The issue, for him, came in the second aspect of the process: actually training the salesmen in how to sell the product. That was hard for him. He had read books about selling, and could talk about sales techniques, but for him it was something he just did. He did not have a structured methodology. He was just himself, and people seemed to buy things from him. He was not sure how it worked. But he recalled enough of the recognised theory and techniques to be able to put together something very credible.

Because of his unease with this talk in particular, his preparation was even more careful than usual. He spent many hours putting together a presentation that would take him about 20 minutes to deliver. He was quite good with PowerPoint, and worked hard to ensure that his talk would be interesting and informative to his high-level audience.

The day came for his presentation. He had

not slept very well the night before, and he felt a few butterflies in his stomach. He did not feel like eating, so skipped breakfast and made himself a strong coffee at home, and then had another when he got to work. As usual, he made sure that he was the first into the room to check that everything was set up right and he was fully prepared by the time the others came in. He connected up the projector to his laptop to make sure that the hardware was all working, and then stared at the big screen in front of him. He clicked for the first slide. Nothing. Next one. Nothing. On and on he went and every slide was blank.

"Don't panic," he thought to himself, "I've just loaded the wrong file." He checked. He had not loaded the wrong file. The data was gone. Hours and hours of work. He took a deep breath and then smiled. He tapped his trouser pocket and felt the memory stick. Before leaving work the previous day he had e-mailed the file to himself at home, in case he wanted to run through it one more time that evening after he got home. As it turned out, he decided not to go through it again, because he had a strong suspicion that running through it at night would interfere with his sleep, and being well rested for the big day was important. Besides, he had rehearsed it many times before. That morning, before leaving home, on an unusual impulse he decided to copy the file onto a memory stick, just in case. Well, now the "just in case" had happened.

He took a deep breath and slotted the stick into his laptop's USB port. He clicked to view its contents. Hooray! There it was – but his blood ran cold as he saw the file size – much too small to be the document that he had based his whole presentation around. He opened it anyway, hoping for a miracle. But there wasn't one. The data was all gone. It must have already been wiped when he had e-mailed it to himself the night before.

His mind whirred with questions and self-criticism. Why hadn't he looked at it the night before? That was really stupid of him. The data was gone. No doubt about it. The original on his office computer must have somehow got corrupted, he copied that onto his laptop, e-mailed it to himself, and copied that onto the memory stick.

His breathing became laboured and he

started to feel dizzy. His heart felt as if it were trying to beat its way out of his chest. He felt terrible. There was something wrong with him, he was sure of it. Was it his heart? He had to get out. He picked up his laptop and bag, and strode quickly towards the door. As he reached it he bumped into John, a colleague and friend. John could see that Peter was in a state, and asked if he was OK.

"No, I'm not. I feel terrible. I've got to go."

"Pete, shall I come with you?"

"No, no… just apologise to everyone for me." And with that he ran out of the building.

His brain was racing. What the hell was happening to him? His mind was not right. Was there something wrong with him mentally? He felt that he was losing control in every way. He was very, very frightened. It was as if something terrible were about to happen. He felt as if he could not get enough air. He jumped into his car, lowered the window, sat back and took deep breaths. It didn't make anything better.

He decided that the problem was not his mind, but his body. There was something wrong with him, really wrong, which was making his mind jumpy. He put his hand on his chest to feel his heart. It seemed to be pounding faster as well as harder. His chest started to feel tight. He needed help urgently. He knew the area well, and drove quickly to the nearby hospital that he knew had an Accident and Emergency department.

He reported to reception, and was told that there was a wait of about an hour and a half. He became distressed at this, and told the triage nurse that he was frightened that there was something wrong with his heart. She looked at him and thought for a moment. "OK, I'll get a doctor to see you as soon as possible." Peter sighed with relief and sat back in the plastic chair. He started to feel himself quietening down. He closed his eyes. He felt relieved. When the doctor arrived, about half an hour later, Peter felt almost embarrassed. He felt a bit shaken up, but actually not that bad. He described what had happened to the doctor, who responded by telling him that it sounded like a panic attack. "But I don't have panic attacks," Peter said. "I don't get panicky... That's not me..."

"Alright," said the doctor, "we'll do an ECG to check that your heart is all OK and do a couple of blood tests, all right?" Peter nodded rapidly. Now they would find out what was wrong with him.

The ECG was thorough, and included monitoring his heart on an exercise bike. "You're as fit as a fiddle. I'd swap hearts with you any day!" the cheerful doctor told him. "We'll send the blood test results through to your GP, but I'm sure they'll show nothing. You, my friend, have just had a panic attack."

The idea that he could have a panic attack was something that had never occurred to Peter, and so he assumed, in the moment of fear, that there was something wrong with his body. This is common for someone experiencing a panic attack – they can't understand why their body is behaving as it is (the pounding heart, feelings of breathlessness etc). Understanding how certain triggers can cause such a reaction is a very helpful first step in overcoming panic.

There is a strong connection here between the workings of the mind and the body. As we will see later, Peter's techniques for recovery addressed both.

Summary of Chapter 2
What is a panic attack?

- A panic attack is a sudden episode of intense overwhelming fear that occurs in a discrete period of time.

- Panic attacks are more likely to occur following distressing experiences and at times of high stress.

- This fear occurs in the absence of a real threat. There is often a sense that something awful is about to happen.

- There is often a desire to escape the situation in which the panic attack is occurring.

- Physical symptoms that occur with the panic attack vary, but will often include feelings of breathlessness, the heart beating harder or faster, light-headedness or dizziness, sweating and chest tightness. There may be abdominal distress, such as nausea or a need to go to the toilet. There may also be odd neurological sensations like shaking or twitching, tingling or numbness in some parts of the body.

- The principal psychological symptom is extreme fear. This may be very general, and hard to attribute to anything specific. Often it will involve dread of a physical disaster, such as having a heart attack, or becoming unable to breathe. Or it might be focused on something more psychological – a compulsion to run away, or a fear of losing control in some way, doing something foolish in front of others. Often the individual may experience a kind of dissociation – a sense that they have become disconnected from themselves or the world.

- Although at the time they may seem to go on for ever, in fact panic attacks often peak in quite a short period of time, typically ten to fifteen minutes, then subside.

- As with anxiety disorders, there are ways to deal with panic attacks that address both mind and body, as we will see later.

CHAPTER 3

WHAT IS AGORAPHOBIA?

PETER'S STORY CONTINUED

A WEEK AFTER HIS VISIT to the A&E department, Peter got the blood test results back from his GP, which were all normal. His doctor raised the hospital's diagnosis of a panic attack with him, but Peter did not accept that as an explanation. To him it was just a weird temporary response that occurred one morning. He must have been unwell, and the unpleasant discovery that he had lost his important data raised his heartbeat enough to tip him over the edge into some horrible physical crisis, which was thankfully short-lived. His GP gave a "whatever" shrug and showed him to the door.

A week later a work commitment meant that Peter had to make a long car journey to Sheffield. He had driven there many times before, and he knew the route well. He had been on the M1 for about an hour, and was listening to the radio. Some tiny thing at the back of his mind registered that he had just passed exit 20, and he knew that the distance to the next exit was the longest on the motorway. That meant that he could not turn round, turn off the road, go back, or do anything except drive on for the next ten or eleven miles. He felt that strange thing happening with his breathing again. He could not get enough air.

He wound down the window and breathed deeply. He felt worse. He looked at his watch. More than ten minutes of this before he could get off the motorway. He glanced in the mirror, saw that there was nothing behind him, so he put his foot down. It was all the same as before: the inability to get air, the pounding heart, the dizziness. He definitely had something really wrong with him. He was feeling more and more frightened. He watched the needle on the speedometer rise from 85 miles per hour to 90, 95, 100 miles per hour. Then he heard the sirens and looked in his rear-view mirror and saw the flashing blue lights. The police. He was being pulled over for speeding.

Even as he slowed down, and indicated to pull into the emergency hard-shoulder lane, he was aware of a curious feeling. He was relieved.

The policeman who got out of the car to talk to him was middle-aged and a little world-weary. When asked what he was doing, Peter blurted out what had happened. But now he was feeling better, he said, though he couldn't tell why. The police officer had seen a lot in his time, and he recognised immediately that Peter was not lying. These were not excuses, nor lies; he was just stating exactly what had happened.

"I think you are having a panic attack, sir," the police officer suggested.

"No, I'm not! I've got something wrong with me – my heart, or breathing or something," Peter protested.

"Well, sounds like a panic attack to me. My missus used to get them. Funnily enough, on the motorway 'specially. Sounds like that to me." Peter just listened in silence. "Anyway, I'm not going to nick you, but I want to escort you off the motorway. We'll drive in front, and you follow, at a safe distance, and leave at the next exit."

Peter was so relieved. "Thank you," he sighed. He was glad to get off the motorway as soon as possible. He fiddled with his satnav and re-programmed it to continue his route avoiding motorways. The trip took him longer, but he didn't feel bad again, and he drove the whole journey back on A-roads. He realised that even the idea of going on a motorway now set off symptoms, albeit to a lesser degree, and he had to admit to himself that there might be something in the panic idea.

The following week he went to the christening of a friend's baby. He was surprised at how many people were there – so many that he had to sit in the middle of a full pew. He looked at the order of service, and saw that the whole thing was going to take much longer than he expected. His breathing went again, his heart thrashed, but he clenched his fists and gritted his teeth, and he got through it. But it was awful. He would never go to a church service again.

Two days later he was queuing in a busy supermarket when he was overtaken by the symptoms. He pushed his trolley to one side and quickly left the shop. As soon as he was outside the symptoms began to subside.

He booked another appointment with his GP, and told him about the motorway, the christening and the supermarket episodes.

"Classic agoraphobia," was the brief answer.

"Agoraphobia *and* panic attacks? What, I've got two things wrong with me now?"

"Well, actually, they often occur together," was the GP's not very encouraging response.

While not the most effusive or helpful of doctors, Peter's GP had at least correctly identified the issues Peter was dealing with – and that meant, with the right support, he could start on the road to recovery.

Agoraphobia and panic attacks are related conditions, and as we will see, there are powerful methods that can be applied for healing both.

Summary of Chapter 3
What is agoraphobia?

- The word agoraphobia comes from the Greek for "fear of the marketplace".

- It is a physical and psychological feeling of fear arising in situations where escape might be difficult.

- Such situations might be literal – for example, being in the car between two exits on a motorway, or being in an aeroplane.

- Or it might be a form of social restriction – such as having to remain in place during a church service, or a play, or standing in a queue in the supermarket.

- It is more likely to occur if there is a feeling that help might not be available in the event of a panic attack.

- There is a strong desire to get out of the

situation, and usually a wish to avoid situations like it in future.

- Often the anxiety is reduced by the presence of a companion, or someone who makes the individual feel safe. (It is interesting to note that Peter started to feel better in the A&E department as soon as he knew that the doctor was coming, and, on the motorway, rather than feeling more anxious when caught speeding, he felt relieved by a sense of safety that came from being with a police officer.)

PART TWO

CHAPTER 4

HEALING: ANXIETY

MICHELLE'S RECOVERY

ON ONE OF HER VISITS to her GP, Michelle asked if she could get some help to deal with her anxiety. Her GP referred her to a cognitive behavioural therapist at a nearby clinic. Michelle felt positive about taking some action. Unfortunately, she had to wait a few months before the appointment came through, but when it did Michelle felt even more determined to change her life.

Her therapist, a woman of roughly the same

age, was called Sally, and seemed to have a practical down-to-earth approach. Michelle liked her. She had been secretly worried that the therapist would ask her lots of questions about her childhood, and try to find some buried secret that didn't exist. But Sally didn't seem to be interested in going down that path. She did take a brief history of Michelle's life, but went on to ask her about her anxieties, how they affected her now, and what her goals were from here. This took Michelle by surprise. In the previous few days she had spent time thinking about the first meeting she would have with her therapist, and how to describe succinctly what was wrong – she had thought a lot about what she *did not* want, but she hadn't really thought much about what she *did* want. When she expressed a negative, such as "I would like to worry less", Sally encouraged her to think of a positive way of reframing that wish.

They arranged a number of meetings over the following three months. Michelle's difficulty with being able to clearly express what she *did* want became her first piece of homework, to be carried out before their next meeting. She was to write a list of goals; things that she wanted. Michelle liked this suggestion. It was something that she could do. For the first time in her life she felt that she was doing something to take control. She knew that it was just the beginning of the story, but nevertheless it felt good. And Sally's positive can-do attitude triggered another unfamiliar feeling in her. She felt optimistic. She could change this. Sally made it clear that it would take work and effort, but that change was certainly possible.

Over the next few days she jotted thoughts down on a piece of paper. At the top she had written simply, "What I would like" and underlined it twice. She kept the list in her handbag, and added to it as ideas came to her over the next few days. By the time that she had her next appointment with Sally, she was really surprised at how long the list was. This is what she wrote down:

1) Be confident that the people I love can stay safe and well

2) Remember that most of the time when I carry out tasks, I get them right

3) Notice when I do things right, and remember it!

4) Use this to help me be more confident about what I have done
5) Sleep well
6) Know that my friends like me
7) Be more confident in social situations
8) Be able to have a good relationship
   [Michelle was aware that she felt anxious as she wrote this one down. She added "good" before relationship as an afterthought]
9) Be able to quieten my mind
10) Be more relaxed in my body
11) Be more interesting
    [A feeling of sadness as she wrote this]
12) Feel sexy
    [High anxiety as she wrote this one]
13) Be physically well
14) Be present in the here and now
    [She was not sure about how to express this one – she knew the negatives; she did not want to keep going over things that had happened in the past or worry about things that might happen in the future, and this wording seemed to be the nearest that she could get]
15) Enjoy travelling
16) See the world

17) Have control
[She double-underlined this one – in a way it seemed to encapsulate everything in two words]
18) Be brave

Michelle typed up the list and brought two copies to her next session with Sally. She felt a little nervous as she passed Sally her copy. Was the list too long? Were there too many things on it? Would Sally think that she had too many problems for them to deal with? The response she got surprised her:

"Michelle, this is fantastic! You have done exactly what we agreed. You have made a list of what you want. It's clear and specific. Gosh, I wish all of my clients could do so well with the first session!"

Michelle smiled, and the seeds of her confidence began to sprout.

Over the next few months they met regularly and Sally helped Michelle to look at her existing beliefs and behaviours, and explore ways of change that moved her towards her goals. Often Sally would give Michelle homework tasks, asking her to write things down, to pay attention to her thinking patterns, notice what was going on when her worrying started, identify any specific triggers to worrying, to consider the worst outcomes, to put things in perspective, and notice the connections with what she was doing and how she was feeling.

Michelle was an enthusiastic and conscientious student. She learned a lot. She learned about the connections between her thinking and her feeling, and how this could become a vicious circle. She learned how her worrying could sometimes become self-fulfilling – that worrying about a job at work the next day meant that she slept badly, and the tiredness the next day meant that she found it harder to concentrate on the task. She learned to differentiate between worries that she could do something about and those that she could not.

Sometimes they would work on particular examples: Michelle had invited a few of her old friends to a barbecue the following weekend. What if it rained? That would spoil everything. Michelle could not influence whether it would rain on the day of her barbecue, but she could influence whether it would spoil everything. She developed a Plan B, what she would do if it rained. She could move the barbecue to the French windows at the back of the living room, and lean out and cook while she and her friends sat inside. It would be fun!

Recognising that worrying about things that she could do nothing about was completely unproductive helped her to let go of these concerns. Recognising that worrying about things that she could do something about could be productive helped her take more control and plan ahead.

With Sally she learned to ask herself, "Is there anything useful about this worry?" Sometimes the answer would be: "yes, because I can take some action to make things better" (like develop a Plan B for the barbecue), but most of the time the answer would be no. Somehow, recognising that the worry was not useful helped Michelle to let go of it.

Visualisation and relaxation

As well as helping Michelle address her thinking patterns, Sally explained that lots of people who suffer anxiety may have a higher baseline level of psycho-physiological arousal than others, and that therefore having some methods to really relax could be useful. Sally took one of their sessions to teach Michelle a couple of simple relaxation and visualisation techniques that she could practise at home. She explained that using the imagination can have a more powerful effect on the body than using words alone.

She asked Michelle to get comfortable and imagine herself standing on a veranda over-looking a beautiful garden. "Imagine to one side of you there is a large ornamental urn with flowers planted in it. You walk over to the urn and you touch it. Feel it... notice what it is made of. Look at the flowers... smell them. You walk along the veranda, and come to a place where there are five steps going down to a beautiful garden below." She asked Michelle to take a long, slow inhalation, take a mental step down and exhale. She asked her to feel herself relaxing more and more deeply with each "step" that she took, so that by the time she was visualising standing on the gravel path at the bottom, she was very deeply relaxed.

She told her to walk along the path and feel the little stones of the gravel crunching under her feet... feel the warmth of the sun on her skin... the gentle breeze. "Perhaps you can hear the leaves rustling in the trees, maybe a bird in the air... and there may be other noises away in the distance, but they don't disturb you, or distract you, because you feel so comfortable and so peaceful here."

Michelle visualised walking down to a stream where the path turned to follow the embankment. She walked along with the stream beside her, looking down into the cool, clear water. She saw patches of bright light reflecting off the surface, between the shade falling from the overhanging trees. And she came to a willow tree, beside which there was a dry grassy hollow. She sat down there and closed her eyes. She felt all the tension draining out of her body... her mind becoming clearer and clearer... more and more peaceful... a lovely feeling of calmness being in this place.

Sally recorded her words as she guided the visualisation exercise, and gave the recording to Michelle as a sound file so that she had something she could use to practise visualisation at home. Sally told Michelle that she could continue to use this recording or could create her own peaceful place in her mind. She might prefer to visualise a beach or a mountain hideaway. She told Michelle that it was helpful for her to draw on all of her senses when imagining the details of her peaceful place – what it looks like, the colours, the shapes, the sounds there, perhaps the gentle waves on water, or the light breeze in the air. She should imagine the feel of wherever she is (such as the sensation of lying on warm grass) and even the smells (of the flowers, for example, or the grass in a meadow). Using her imagination in this way would help Michelle trigger a relaxation response.

Sally taught Michelle other methods too – for example, having reached a relaxed state, she could visualise putting all her worries into a cardboard box, and then dumping that box into a bin to be taken away with the rubbish. Or writing her concerns on pieces of paper and then dropping them into a stream and watching them drift away until they were out of sight.

Another technique that they implemented was progressive muscle relaxation. Sally told Michelle to sit back in her chair and close her eyes. She asked her to stay there quietly for a few minutes, simply paying attention to her breathing – her lips together, breathing through her nose and low down into her abdomen, just noticing the air going in and out of her body.

Sally observed Michelle quieten physically, then asked her to wiggle her shoulders to loosen up for the exercise. She wanted Michelle to pay attention to the different muscle groups in her body, starting with the top of her head and going downwards. Following Sally's instructions, Michelle began by focussing on her scalp, feeling for any tension there and consciously letting it go, before moving on to the little muscles around her eyes – again just letting them loosen. Sally suggested it might help to imagine the muscles changing colour as they relaxed, or noticing a feeling of warmth.

Michelle carried this down through the muscles of her head and neck, down through the shoulders, continuing that loosening and relaxation, down through her arms, right to the tips of her fingers. Michelle noticed, in particular, a sense of heaviness in her arms and hands. She then moved on to the muscles in her chest and her back, and pictured that same relaxation going through her whole body – down through her hips and thighs and knees, down through her calves and ankles to the tips of her toes. And then she just rested there, paying attention to that feeling, the physical relaxation and sense of peace.

It took them about ten minutes to work through this exercise and when they were done Michelle felt considerably more relaxed. Sally recommended doing progressive muscle relaxation at home before a visualisation exercise, and explained that most people find that they get better at the technique with practice. She also told Michelle that some people find they are helped by listening to a voice-guided relaxation soundtrack, using a mindfulness app or playing some peaceful, relaxing music.

Tackling catastrophic thinking

Having given Michelle some techniques that she could practise away from their meetings, Sally returned to Michelle's thinking patterns, and helped her to recognise when she was "catastrophising" – imagining the worst possible outcome of any particular event. What if she does put some papers in the wrong file, or the washing machine does leak? These things create annoyances or inconveniences, but they are not catastrophes, and Michelle began to learn to put such things into perspective. They paid attention to the likelihood of certain negative things happening. What if she travelled abroad and something happened that stopped her getting home? Sally asked her, "Has that ever happened to you?"

"No."

"Do you know anyone that it has happened to?"

"Well, yes. My friend Jane was in America when the volcano in Iceland erupted and released the ash cloud, and she couldn't get home."

"And is she still there?"

Michelle laughed. "Of course not! She got home about a week later."

"So even when there was some very unusual event that left somebody stuck where they were for a little while, they just came home a bit later?"

Michelle smiled again. "You're right – in the big scheme of things it didn't really matter, did it?" It was an inconvenience, not a catastrophe.

Michelle reinforced her learning to take

action on the worries that she could do something about, and to let go of those that were beyond her control. Gradually she developed a habit of thinking in this way. Once she realised that worrying about such things was of no use to her, it was easier to let go of them.

She learned that there were some things that she could control and some that she could not, but actually that was OK. The world was not always predictable, and she could not control everything, and sometimes things did go wrong. But they were rarely catastrophic, and things usually worked out in the end.

Alongside the change in her thinking patterns, Sally encouraged Michelle to modify her behaviour patterns too – not to avoid situations, but work out a strategy for enlarging the world that she moved in. This was done step by step, and sometimes demanded courage, but facing up to her fears and making the changes gave Michelle a confidence that she had not felt before. She decided to go on a holiday in Scotland with her friends, and she loved it. Her friends were struck by how positive and confident she was becoming, and when they asked her to come on a girls' long weekend to

Marbella, she surprised herself by saying yes immediately.

Other techniques

Sally also taught Michelle a few tricks for managing worry. For example she could assign a certain time of day for worrying – perhaps from 6.30pm to 7.00pm. If she found herself worrying during the day she could tell herself that this was not the right time, and attend instead to what she was doing. Increasingly, Michelle found that when the allotted time arrived she forgot to worry, or that the thing seemed to be less important than it was some hours earlier.

Another simple method was distraction: carrying out some task at home, calling or, better still, going to visit a friend often takes the mind away from an anxious thought and helps restore perspective and a feeling of calmness.

Another option was practising acceptance: "OK – here is this thought again. I have had it lots of times before. It's not nice but it doesn't actually harm me – and I know that after a short time it will just drift by." When Sally talked to Michelle about this one, she added that she could use her visualisation and picture the anxious thought like a cloud and watch it drift by in the bright blue sky.

Assertiveness

To help her feel more confident in social situations they worked on assertiveness. Michelle was anxious about this at first, because she associated the idea with being aggressive or pushy. Sally explained that assertiveness was neither of these things, and in fact was completely different – so they looked at it in more detail.

> *There are two unhelpful ways in which people can respond to a situation of stress or conflict – they might get aggressive, or they might back down and give up. Assertiveness, however, is not just something between these two extremes; it is altogether different.*
>
> *The rules of assertive communication are very simple, and very effective – and all too rarely used! The most important principle of assertive communication is that the person expresses*

what they are feeling, and what they want. In common language assertiveness is sometimes confused with aggression. Aggressive statements often start with "You…" and go on to say something unpleasant about the other person "…are stupid / selfish / horrible…" Assertive statements do not generally say anything about the other person, but about what the speaker is feeling.

Here are the simple rules for an assertive statement:

1) *Start it with "I". This will set you off down the right path!*
2) *Say something about what you are feeling: "I feel sad / anxious / concerned…"*
3) *Say what the feeling is about: "I feel anxious when people shout at me…" (Aggressive statements, in contrast, usually say something about the other person – "you are really annoying" etc.)*
4) *Say what you would like from the other person: "I feel anxious when people shout at me, so I would like you to talk quietly to me…"*
5) *Ask for their agreement. "Will you do that please?" Good assertive communication*

tends to get good results. It can also help get clarity – if the other person replies, "No, I won't do that", then the response is "Could you explain to me why not?" There is no blaming or attacking, but an expression of what one person would like to happen, and if that is not granted, a request for clarity about the situation.

Michelle was not sure about this. Then she thought about her friends, and the ones that she liked the most were actually the ones who seemed naturally assertive. She tried it out when she was meeting up with a friend for a meal. Michelle did something unfamiliar – she said what she wanted. "I really fancy a Chinese, would that be OK for you?"

"Fine," said her friend, and they had a great time together.

Michelle thus achieved two things: she got what she wanted, but perhaps more importantly, she gave herself a message – that her feelings, and what she wanted, were significant and had value. She practised this style of communication, and a short while later something happened at work. She had had a toothache for a couple of days, and it was getting worse. Painkillers stopped providing relief, and she called her dentist. There was an appointment available that day at 4.30pm. Michelle booked it, and then realised something: in all her years at work she had never once left early. Could she ask her boss if she could do that? She took a deep breath and went to see him.

"John, I have really bad toothache, and I need to go to the dentist. He has a space at 4.30 this afternoon, so I would like to go then, which would mean leaving a little early. Would you be OK with that?"

John smiled, "Michelle, you are one of the most reliable people I have ever met. If you need to leave early, you leave early. In fact, if you are really suffering, go home now if you want."

What a surprise for Michelle – she was anxious about asking for something, and ended up with a compliment and feeling valued. Again she was giving herself a message – what she was feeling was important and had value.

At work her confidence grew. She learned that she could say to her boss "Sorry, I haven't had time to finish this today", or "I can't find the file right now", and nothing bad happened. She would finish the work the next day, and find the file in the afternoon. It was all right. There was, in fact, very little to worry about. In short, rather than feel that her life was being governed by a sequence of external events over which she had little control, Michelle was learning to take charge of her life.

Michelle's healing process shows that challenging habitual patterns of negative thinking and behaviour can make a big difference in overcoming an anxiety disorder. It does take some effort, but by thinking positively about what we want, understanding why the mind and body react the way they do to certain triggers, practising relaxation techniques such as mindfulness, visualisation or progressive muscle relaxation, and being more assertive about our views can all help in regaining control over a situation.

The summary points highlight the key things someone suffering from anxiety can do or take into consideration when on the road to recovery, and you can refer back to Michelle's story to see how she addressed these points with her therapist, Sally.

Summary of Chapter 4
Healing: anxiety

- If you have any concerns about your physical health, see your GP.

- If necessary, get professional help from an experienced therapist.

- Think positively about what you would like. It might be helpful to write a list.

- Know that change is possible.

- Find ways to take control.

- Become aware of existing beliefs and behaviour patterns.

- Notice triggers to worrying, and the connections with what you are doing and how you are feeling.

- Identify the worst outcomes, put things in perspective – consider the likelihood of various outcomes, and whether or not they are truly catastrophic.

- Negative thinking and feeling bad can become a vicious circle.

- Identify which worries you can do something about and which you cannot.

- Learn to let go of those worries that you can do nothing about.

- For the worries you can do something about – make plans and create change by taking action.

- Learn a relaxation technique. Using visualisation or progressive muscle relaxation is likely to be helpful (see Sally's guidance for Michelle on pages 73-78).

- You can use visualisation to picture yourself dumping your worries (see page 76).

- It may be helpful to assign a specific time in your day for addressing your worries, and to postpone all your worrying until then (see page 81). When the time comes around, you may have forgotten the worries you had earlier, or may see them from a more objective and reasoned perspective.

- Be adventurous. One step at a time, change patterns of behaviour. Notice when things go well.

- Learn assertive communication (pages 82-84).

- Just as anxiety can become a negative cycle, so changing the way you deal with potential problems can become a positive one. A different approach can result in a better outcome, and because of that you feel more confident for the next issue you face, and so on. Consequently, you can take more and more control of your life.

CHAPTER 5

HEALING: PANIC
AND AGORAPHOBIA

PETER'S RECOVERY

"So what do I need to do? Is there some medication for this?" Peter asked his GP hopefully. "It would be so good if there were a pill to fix it."

"We don't really recommend medication for panic problems, certainly not in the first instance. You need to see a psychologist."

Peter was lucky to be senior enough in his company to receive health insurance as a benefit. This enabled him to get to see an experienced psychologist within a week. His name was Andrew, and he had been working in the field for 25 years, making a speciality of dealing with panic attacks. Andrew took detailed notes of Peter's story, including information about his physical health, and expressed confidence that they would get him back in control within a few weeks. He made an appointment to see Peter again, a few days later.

At the second meeting, Andrew asked Peter about his recent bereavement. Peter was not expecting this question, but began to talk about his grandmother. Once he started, he found himself pouring out thoughts about her, and surprised himself by shedding some tears as he talked about her loss. Andrew quietly passed him a box of tissues, giving him as much time as he needed. "I suppose I just pushed the sadness away... I had the presentation to work on... I kind of pushed it to the back of my mind," Peter admitted.

Andrew explained that it was not unusual for panic attacks to start following a bereavement or other emotional trauma, and said that it was more likely to become a problem when feelings were suppressed and there was no outlet for real grieving. Peter listened with an open mind, but wondered how all of this actually fit together.

At the next session, Andrew asked Peter about the earlier bereavement of his other grandmother, just before he took his A-levels. Again, Peter was surprised by the line of enquiry, but he went with it. "Well, she died suddenly, just before my exams…" Again a few tears rolled down his cheeks. "And I had to keep revising… I had to stay focused, to keep going… But it was all a bit pointless really…"

"Just take a moment and let yourself feel what's there… whatever wants to come out…"

Although this felt strange and unfamiliar to him, he gave room for his emotions. After a few minutes he felt tears running down his cheeks. He wept for a short time. Then he settled, and his body calmed. Andrew picked up from where they had paused: "You were saying it was a bit pointless… why was that?"

"Because I screwed up anyway."

"What happened?"

"Well, in the first one, geography…" Andrew noticed Peter's breathing getting deeper and faster as he thought back to the exam. "Well, I turned the paper over, looked at the questions, realised that there were one or two that I would struggle with… and then…"

"Then what?"

"Then my mind went blank… Gosh, I'd forgotten… I felt really terrible… like the other day in the office…"

Andrew nodded silently.

"It was the same, wasn't it? It was a panic attack then?"

"Sounds like it, Peter. And let's just look at the parallels. You lose a loved family member. You have to do some important piece of work. There is no time for your grief, so you bury it. But it makes your heart beat a bit faster, and your breathing quicken. Just a few minutes ago, did you notice how much your body reacted when you felt the sadness of your loss?"

Peter nodded.

"This time, here, we paused, and you let those tears go, and then your body settled down."

Another thoughtful nod.

"But in the two situations that we're talking about, you were not able to express the emotion, and the physical disturbance remained. Does that make sense?"

"Yes, I think it does."

"And carrying that disturbance along with you, you are then faced with a work task and something goes wrong... The question on the paper is not what you expected, or you have lost the data for your presentation. I suspect that under other circumstances you would have been able to manage, but at these two times when you had the physiological disturbance of the contained grief, combined with the psychological experience of stress, you got into a spin, your thinking was impaired – that made you feel panicky, which made thinking more difficult, and so on."

Andrew explained that Peter's body would have been going into an alarm "get me out of here" mode. When Peter said that he did not remember thinking such a thing, Andrew explained that these switches were not thrown by any conscious thought, but by some more primitive mechanism – a reaction to fear.

Andrew also pointed out that, on the morning of the presentation, Peter had skipped breakfast, which would have left his blood sugar levels low. And then he drank coffee, the caffeine in which would have helped precipitate the physical symptoms of panic.

"So what can I do about it, if it's not conscious?" Peter asked.

"Good question. And the answer is regain control."

"How do I do that?"

Andrew went on to explain that panic attacks occur as an interaction between mind and body. "A part of the brain sends out an alarm signal, the body responds, we feel the reaction, the reaction frightens us, more alarm signals get sent out, and round we go."

"So what do I do about it?"

"Well, as panic is a consequence of an inter-action between mind and body, it makes sense that to fix things we need to look at both. The easiest one to start with is the body. I believe that not knowing what is going on makes things worse, and conversely, understanding the process helps reduce the cycle of fear. So what I suggest is that first of all I explain some of the physiology to you, then I give you some simple exercises to do over the next week or two. This gives you something that you can use right away, from the moment you leave this room, and will quickly give you back some control. Then we will take a few sessions to pay attention to what is going on in your mind."

Peter felt relieved just hearing this. He was not going mad and he wasn't dying of a heart problem – it was simply that, for some reason, his mind and body, in combination, were over-reacting to something. And, most importantly, it was something he could learn to control.

The importance of breathing

"Peter, you mentioned to me that when you had the episodes you felt as if you couldn't get enough air… I think that, in fact, you were hyperventilating. You were over-breathing. It goes with panic."

"But I couldn't get *enough* air."

"I understand that, Peter. I understand that it felt as if you were not breathing enough. But there are logical reasons why over-breathing can make us feel that way."

Peter looked confused.

"OK, Peter, just bear with me. Let me explain the physiology, and then I would like us to do an experiment, so that we can see if your breathing affects how you are feeling. Would that be OK?"

Peter told Andrew he was open to trying whatever he had in mind.

"Breathing is one of the most powerful ways to influence your physiology," Andrew explained, "and thus the most powerful way to help break into the vicious cycle between mind and body, so that you calm your body, calm your mind and gain control. People sometimes find it hard to believe that changing the way you breathe can have such a massive impact on the way you feel. But it really can.

"There are two reasons why I teach people breathing exercises as a way into the body. First, how we breathe has a knock-on effect on numerous other physiological systems. This can work both ways – if we breathe badly it can negatively impact those other systems, but conversely, if we breathe well, it can improve their function. The second reason is related to voluntary control. For most of us it would be pretty hard to just choose to slow our heart rate, or lower our blood pressure, or decrease our sweating – but we can change our breathing pattern. We can breathe faster or slower, deeper or shallower, and how we are breathing will have an effect on our heart rate, sweating and so on. So it is a powerful way into the body. If you want to control your heart rate, control your breathing.

"The evidence that breathing control helps in overcoming panic attacks is very strong. The primary reason why how we breathe has such a powerful effect on how we feel in respect of multiple bodily systems is that it affects the chemistry of the blood, changing the delicate balance of oxygen and carbon dioxide in it. Everyone knows that we need oxygen to survive, and people sometimes tell you to take lots of deep breaths if you are feeling stressed or anxious – and this was your instinct when you were feeling bad before the meeting, and when you were on the motorway. But this is not a good idea. In fact, it is most likely to make you feel worse."

Peter raised his eyebrows. He had made himself worse?

Andrew continued: "We have a relatively wide range of tolerance to levels of oxygen in the blood, and a relatively low tolerance to changes in the level of carbon dioxide. This is because carbon dioxide is acidic in solution, and small changes in carbon dioxide levels change the acid–alkaline balance of the blood. Because the blood goes everywhere and affects every organ, the effects of such adjustments can produce changes throughout the body.

"When we are stressed by something – like finding that our PowerPoint data has been lost – it is normal for respiration to increase in rate and depth as part of an alarm response. With you, for whatever reason, which we will find in the next session or two, that response went into overdrive. The process of over-breathing causes an excess of carbon dioxide to be released from the blood, which makes the blood more alkaline, precipitating some key changes throughout the body. There are five that are really important:

"Firstly, your heart rate goes up – you certainly felt that one.

"Secondly, there is an effect on the way that nerve cells fire, so that initially they may be triggered more easily, but eventually become underactive. This may be experienced symp-tomatically as pins and needles or numbness, and subjectively as having 'too much' energy – feeling nervy and jumpy (perhaps involving twitching or a temporary tremor). This will eventually flip into a feeling of having too little energy – of feeling exhausted.

"The next change is the most complex and superficially counter-intuitive piece of chemistry in this process – it is the effect of oxygen dissociation. Haemoglobin in the blood carries the oxygen. If the blood is more alkaline it releases oxygen to the tissues less easily. Over-breathing, typically associated with panic, reduces the level of carbon dioxide in the blood, making it a bit more alkaline. So the paradox of this piece of biochemistry is that in over-breathing we are actually making less oxygen available to the body. This is probably why you had the subjective feeling that you were not getting enough air. If we want to make more oxygen available, we need to slow the breathing, which will raise the carbon dioxide level, correcting the acid–alkaline balance of the blood, and helping the haemoglobin to release oxygen where it is needed.

"So, fourth on the list is that fact that the change in blood chemistry causes vasoconstriction – the arteries narrow down. Peter, for you this process in itself is not dangerous – but it can cause some disturbing physical sensations.

It may result in poor blood flow to the extremities, but for most people the important area is the head. Over-breathing can very significantly reduce blood flow to the brain, and this is one of the main reasons why you might feel light-headed or dizzy at these times, and why clear thinking can sometimes be impaired. Being aware that your thinking is impaired can escalate stress (for example when you need to make a presentation to your bosses, and you have lost the data you needed). It can alarm you more, and escalate the vicious circle between mind and body stress. That is, unless we have a management strategy.

"And finally, and perhaps not surprisingly, when you combine the interference in nerve cell function, the reduction in oxygen availability and the reduction in blood flow to the brain, over-breathing produces a massive change in brain wave patterns. This is probably why people struggle to think clearly when they get very stressed, finding it difficult to see the bigger picture, and maintain complex rational thought processes. The end product is most commonly fear, and because our brains cannot work that well under these conditions, we sometimes have difficulty in engaging our rational minds to put things in perspective.

"Oh, and also the way that people typically breathe when they are stressed (high up in the chest) may irritate the muscles between the ribs, causing them to tighten up. This can lead to a feeling of tightness in the chest and difficulty in taking a 'full' breath – all sensations that you mentioned feeling.

"One last point – the disturbances in psychological functioning brought about by over-breathing can sometimes lead people to feel that they are losing control of their thinking – which is of course very unpleasant, and maintains and escalates the cycle between a body going into alarm mode and an anxious mind."

Breathing technique

Wow, there was an explanation for everything that Peter had been feeling! This realisation was making him feel a lot better already.

Andrew then told Peter he would like to try the experiment he had mentioned earlier, to see if they could observe any relationship between Peter's breathing and how he was feeling. From the first session, he already knew that Peter was generally healthy, and did not suffer from any ailment such as heart, respiratory or neurological problems, so he was safe to conduct this test with him. Andrew initially asked Peter to take rapid deep breaths, as if he were puffed out. He asked him to do this for a minute, glancing occasionally at the second hand of his watch. Peter started off fine, but within 30 seconds felt terrible. His heart was pounding, and he felt dizzy – just like during the episodes. He stopped panting. Andrew suggested that he take a couple of minutes to let things settle. They both agreed that this simple test demonstrated a very real relationship between Peter's breathing and the production of symptoms that he experienced during the panic episodes.

Then Andrew offered to show Peter a breathing technique that he could follow. He placed one hand on his abdomen and one higher up over his breastbone. He kept his mouth closed and breathed slowly low down so that only his lower hand was moving. Peter followed him well. Within five minutes he felt so peaceful that he could almost doze off! He had not felt so calm in ages. Peter did not need any more convincing. How he breathed radically affected how he felt.

Andrew gave him a printed sheet of instructions for breathing exercises to be carried out between their meetings:

Breathing from the diaphragm is the most natural and relaxing way to breathe at rest. When we are stressed or anxious the abdominal muscles can tighten and inhibit this calm breathing mode, so the first thing to do is check where you are breathing from.

Step 1. Loosen your clothing and lie on your back, with a cushion under your head. Place one hand flat down on your abdomen, so that your thumb is just below the bottom of your ribcage. Place the other hand palm down on the middle of your breastbone. Now notice where you are breathing from. You should feel your lower hand gently rising as you inhale, and falling as you exhale, with very little movement in your upper hand.

Step 2. This is to get the rate of breathing right. Still lying down, keeping your lips together, and teeth apart, just take a couple of minutes to notice the air going in and out of your nose.

Avoid breathing in or out through your mouth. There is not a rate of respiration that is perfect for everybody – we have different lung capacities, and different physiology – but the following will be about right for most people. Breathing only low down, and not inflating your chest, inhale for a count of three, and exhale for a count of four. Do not hold your breath, but if it feels comfortable, you can pause for a second or two at the end of an exhalation.

Practise this often, even if only for a few minutes at a time. Do it in bed at night before going to sleep. If you wake in the night do it for a short while and you will calm your physiology enough to help you go back to sleep. Take a few minutes to do the exercise at the beginning of your day to get yourself off to a better start. At various times during the day take a minute or two out, sit back and breathe from your diaphragm. After a while this will become a natural pattern for you.

Getting the breathing going calmly from the right place helps put you back in control, and gives the brain a message that you are relaxed. If you feel some of the panicky symptoms starting up, use the breathing technique. The more you practise it when you feel all right, the easier it will be to switch it on if you start to feel uncomfortable. Generally, the sooner you can catch it, the more effectively you will block the spiral of panic before it gets going.

How panic happens

In the next two or three sessions they went on to look at some of Peter's beliefs about panic. One of them was that if he hadn't escaped the situation that had triggered the symptoms – by running out of the conference room, or getting off the motorway – things would have worsened until something terrible happened. Andrew explained that this belief, though apparently intuitive, was incorrect. The truth is that the symptoms of panic peak and then decline – which is actually exactly what Peter experienced. A panic attack is naturally self-limiting; the decline and cessation of the panic will occur spontaneously whether the person removes themselves from a situation or not.

Andrew questioned Peter further about his interpretation of what he had felt was happening to him when he was having a panic attack. Peter found it a little difficult to put into words, but with some encouragement he was able to pin down the more frightening thoughts that had assailed his mind: namely that something was seriously wrong with him – with his heart, or lungs or brain.

"When I felt that bad in the conference room, my instinct was that I just had to run out – I didn't have any choice. Something made me do it. I thought there was something wrong with my body or I was losing my mind. I was going to die or go mad."

Peter's problem, which is typical in a panic attack, was that he had very unpleasant symptoms without having any explanation for them. As a result, his mind took him to the most catastrophic possibilities, which escalated his fear and the vicious cycle of increasing anxiety and increasing physical symptoms. Understanding this process was an important part of the therapy – and now Peter could see why. He learned that if he started to feel the onset of any symptoms he could remind himself of what was actually going on – that his body was overreacting to something, like an over-sensitive alarm going off to a tiny stimulus –

rather than let further worries about his health and wellbeing pile on top of each other. He learned that he could use breathing techniques to settle his physiology, and could tell himself that while the situation might feel unpleasant, it was not a disaster. He knew now that what was happening could just be a reflection of his general sensitivity, and the negative feeling would fade quite soon anyway.

Peter also learned that avoidance of a situation is generally not a good thing. Most of the time fear responses are learned faster than they are unlearned, so we have to expose ourselves to the feared situation to realise that we can take control and can cope with the outcome. To do this you do not have to throw yourself in at the deep end. The best way to achieve it is in a series of graduated steps.

Andrew got Peter to make a list of situations that he might find difficult, ranging from those eliciting only a little anxiety, to those provoking the most. Peter made two lists, one for driving and one for presentations. For the driving list, he rated driving from home to work as a zero – it created no anxiety for him – while driving on a long stretch of motorway with no exits, or through a long tunnel, was the situation that would trigger the most stress. For the presentations, his list started with the low anxiety of chatting with his team, and peaked at presenting to the board. With Andrew he worked out the steps in between – driving on long stretches of dual carriageway, or presenting to his peers and at trade conferences.

Over the next few weeks, Peter used the techniques that he had learned – understanding what was going on with his mind and body, challenging catastrophic thinking and replacing these thoughts with more rational interpretations of events, using his breathing to manage his physiology, and working his way up through the list that he had made with Andrew. He actually advanced up the list without difficulty. With each item that he tackled his confidence grew.

Two months later he had to drive along the same piece of motorway where he had had the panic attack. He smiled with pleasure as he enjoyed the sense of achievement in overcoming his agoraphobic feeling. He was back in the driving seat of his mind as well as his car.

Another month later he had to make his

quarterly presentation to the top bosses. He experienced a little apprehension at first, but he calmed himself with his breathing, and remembered how well he had done with other presentations recently. He was touched by one or two of the directors asking after his health – these people were thoughtful human beings just like him! His initial nerves quickly faded and he gave the most confident presentation of his career.

As with Michelle's experiences, Peter's healing process involved a set of simple changes that had a big effect on his body and mind – in his case, positively impacting how he reacted to situations that might otherwise have led to panic.

By expressing our feelings and practising breathing techniques as Peter did, as well as addressing the same issues that Michelle faced concerning anxiety and catastrophic thinking, we can recover from and ultimately prevent panic attacks. Knowing that panic attacks are naturally self-limiting means we can learn not to avoid circumstances that have triggered them in the past. By gradually exposing ourselves to such situations, we can learn that we are not in danger and can become free of panic.

The summary points highlight the key things someone suffering from panic attacks and agoraphobia can do or take into consideration when on the road to recovery, and you can refer back to Peter's story, and also to Michelle's, to see how they addressed these matters with their therapists.

Summary of Chapter 5
Healing: panic and agoraphobia

- If you have any concerns about your physical health, see your GP.

- If necessary, get professional help from an experienced therapist.

- People who have panic attacks are generally more sensitive or anxious than others. Dealing with panic attacks will often require dealing with the issues in Michelle's story (chapter 1) and her recovery (chapter 4) so as to reduce the baseline level of physiological arousal.

- Panic is more likely to occur following bereavement or other stressful events.

- Containing feeling, rather than expressing it, may be more likely to lead to panic. Expressing contained feeling, for example by crying when we feel sad, can help to restore the body's calmness.

- Sometimes a pattern of events that reminds us of a previous experience that led to panic can trigger a reaction.

- Panic is the result of an interaction between mind and body, therefore it makes sense to aim therapy at both places.

- Panic impairs thinking.

- Understanding what is happening to the body and mind is usually helpful.

- Panic usually involves a feeling of being out of control either physically or emotionally, or both.

- Over-breathing is usually the principal physiological cause of escalating panic. (See pages 99-103 for details on the disruption of the acid–alkaline levels in the blood caused by over-breathing.)

- Therefore, using breathing techniques to gain control of respiration will help to prevent the vicious cycle between body and mind developing. Learning to control breathing will take a little practice, but will be a great benefit. (See pages 105-107 for the technique Andrew taught Peter.)

- The mind can be managed by challenging catastrophic thinking. Events can be unpleasant, annoying, upsetting, but they are rarely catastrophic. (See pages 78-79 for Sally's advice to Michelle.)

- Panic attacks are typically self-limiting to around 10–15 minutes. So do not avoid situations that you have found difficult in the past. This gives you a chance to learn to be more confident remaining in the previously stressful environment. Write out a hierarchy of situations that have caused feelings of panic and work your way through it, starting with what is easiest and moving on to what feels more difficult for you at the moment (through this measured approach, the later situations will get easier over time). In this way, your mind can un-learn the fear response that you might have had in the past.

- Do not skip meals – a low blood sugar level can increase the likelihood of panicky feelings in some people.

- Give up caffeinated drinks – caffeine is present in most colas, some medications, many of the "energy" drinks and, of course, coffee.

- Anxiety and panic can worsen if the mind is not occupied. Finding something to do, however simple, will often provide not just a means of distraction, but also a feeling of having some level of control.

LOOKING AHEAD

Two YEARS AFTER HER FIRST meeting with Sally, Michelle felt like a completely different person. She looked back at the "wish list" that she had made after their first session and realised just how much she'd changed. Now she felt more relaxed; she was confident, in both work situations and social and romantic relationships (in fact she had just got engaged). She was able to really enjoy being in the present without fretting as she used to about what she might have said earlier or what might happen at work the next day. She was enjoying travelling, and became the one who encouraged her friends to choose more adventurous destinations (her most recent suggestion was to go to Sumatra to see orang-utans). She was more assertive in her dealings with people, and was generally positive and optimistic.

For Peter, a year after his first meeting with Andrew, remembering how he felt at that time was like a dream, it seemed so far away now. He learned to express his feelings rather than contain them. He had learned that coffee was not for him, and he no longer skipped meals. He knew that he could control his physiology with his breathing exercises, and ironically, the confidence that this gave him meant that he hardly ever felt the need to use them. He no longer experienced catastrophic thinking patterns. He did not avoid anything because of anxiety. He could drive on any motorway, through any tunnel, without the slightest glimmer of a problem. When he had to make an important presentation, he sometimes noticed a physical reaction in his body. Rather than experience this as anxiety, he now felt it as a sign of excitement. Instead of leading to panic, this, he knew, would give him an edge.

It is interesting to note that both Peter and Michelle are sensitive people. There is nothing wrong with this; in fact, in many ways this is a positive attribute. Sensitivity to others can help make us good partners, parents and workers. But one of the disadvantages of sensitivity is that it may leave us more vulnerable to different kinds of anxiety. That is not a disaster, but simply means that sensitive people may need more conscious strategies for managing their feelings than their less sensitive friends and colleagues.

The key achievement for both Michelle and Peter is that they learned to gain control. They gained control of their emotions, their physiology and their psychology, and in doing so successfully overcame anxiety and panic.

By taking an unpleasant experience of anxiety or panic, and approaching it constructively, learning to understand what makes us react and behave the way we do, it is possible to gain a greater degree of awareness and confidence than we have ever experienced before.

Further resources

The British Psychological Society has information about psychology, and how to find a psychologist. www.bps.org.uk

The United Kingdom Council for Psycho-therapy provides information about therapy and lists of qualified therapists. www.psycho-therapy.org.uk

The British Association for Behavioural and Cognitive Therapies provides information about cognitive behavioural therapy and a register of their accredited therapists. www.babcp.com

The Health and Care Professions Council regulates a number of healthcare professions including practitioner psychologists, and enables individuals to confirm that a

psychologist is registered with an indepen-
dent body. www.hpc-uk.org

Mind is a mental health charity that provides
information about mental health issues and
advice and support to help anyone experiencing
a mental health problem. Mind campaigns to
improve services, raise awareness and promote
understanding. www.mind.org.uk

**The British Association for Counselling
& Psychotherapy (BACP)** sets standards for
therapeutic practice and provides information for therapists, clients of therapy, and the
general public. www.bacp.co.uk

Acknowledgements

I would like to thank: Judith for planting the seed that grew into this series of books, at Short Books, Clemmie for being a great catalyst, Aurea for her ideas and her faith in the process, and Paul for his astute observations; my wonderful children, Emily, Joe and Cathy for teaching me so much about life, and helping to keep me sane; Nila, for everything that you have brought to me; two respected colleagues and valued friends – Dr Brian Roet and Dr Niall Campbell, for their support both professional and personal over many years, and finally to the clients that I have worked with, who have had the courage to share their stories and make these books possible, I say thank you.